W9-ATA-179

CELEBRATING HOLIDAYS

Thanksgiving

by Rachel Grack

BLASTOFF!
2
READERS

BELLWETHER MEDIA • MINNEAPOLIS, MN

Note to Librarians, Teachers, and Parents:

Blastoff! Readers are carefully developed by literacy experts and combine standards-based content with developmentally appropriate text.

Level 1 provides the most support through repetition of high-frequency words, light text, predictable sentence patterns, and strong visual support.

Level 2 offers early readers a bit more challenge through varied simple sentences, increased text load, and less repetition of high-frequency words.

Level 3 advances early-fluent readers toward fluency through increased text and concept load, less reliance on visuals, longer sentences, and more literary language.

Level 4 builds reading stamina by providing more text per page, increased use of punctuation, greater variation in sentence patterns, and increasingly challenging vocabulary.

Level 5 encourages children to move from "learning to read" to "reading to learn" by providing even more text, varied writing styles, and less familiar topics.

Whichever book is right for your reader, Blastoff! Readers are the perfect books to build confidence and encourage a love of reading that will last a lifetime!

This edition first published in 2017 by Bellwether Media, Inc.

No part of this publication may be reproduced in whole or in part without written permission of the publisher. For information regarding permission, write to Bellwether Media, Inc., Attention: Permissions Department, 5357 Penn Avenue South, Minneapolis, MN 55419.

Library of Congress Cataloging-in-Publication Data

Names: Koestler-Grack, Rachel A., 1973- author.
Title: Thanksgiving / by Rachel Grack.
Description: Minneapolis, MN : Bellwether Media, Inc., 2017. | Series: Blastoff! Readers: Celebrating Holidays | Includes bibliographical references and index. | Audience: Ages: 5-8. | Audience: Grades: K to Grade 3.
Identifiers: LCCN 2016035470 (print) | LCCN 2016036356 (ebook) | ISBN 9781626175983 (hardcover : alkaline paper) | ISBN 9781681033280 (ebook)
Subjects: LCSH: Thanksgiving Day–Juvenile literature.
Classification: LCC GT4975 .K64 2017 (print) | LCC GT4975 (ebook) | DDC 394.2649-dc23
LC record available at https://lccn.loc.gov/2016035470

Editor: Christina Leaf   Designer: Lois Stanfield

Printed in the United States of America, North Mankato, MN.

Table of Contents

Thanksgiving Is Here!

Corn and squash steam on the table. A **cornucopia** overflows with vegetables and fruits.

cornucopia

Finally, the turkey is done roasting. Thanksgiving dinner is ready!

What Is Thanksgiving?

Thanksgiving is a **national** holiday in the United States.

Families gather together to feast. They show thanks for what they have.

Who Celebrates Thanksgiving?

Thanksgiving is mainly a United States holiday. Most Americans celebrate it.

Montreal,
Canada

Canadians hold their own
Thanksgiving. It happens
in October.

Thanksgiving Beginnings

Thanksgiving came from a **harvest** celebration in 1621. It happened in the Plymouth **Colony** of Massachusetts.

Pilgrims and the **Wampanoag** people feasted together. The Wampanoag had helped the Pilgrims grow crops.

Massachusetts

N
W E
S

Massachusetts

Plymouth

The harvest **festival** lasted three days. They ate **venison**, duck, and corn pudding.

venison

actors playing
Pilgrims

They held shooting contests
and ran races.

Thanksgiving became a
national holiday in 1863.

Today, Americans celebrate on the fourth Thursday in November. President Franklin D. Roosevelt made this rule in 1941.

President Franklin D. Roosevelt

Thanksgiving Traditions!

Today's Thanksgiving foods are different than those in 1621. Families eat stuffing, mashed potatoes, and turkey. Pumpkin pie is a favorite dessert.

pumpkin pie

Indian Pudding

This cornmeal dish is similar to foods that the Pilgrims and Wampanoag ate. Have an adult help you with this recipe.

Recipe

What You Need:

- 1 tablespoon butter
- 2 cups milk
- ½ cup half & half
- ¾ cup cornmeal
- 2 eggs
- ½ cup molasses

- saucepan
- small baking dish
- measuring cups
- large spoon
- small bowl
- fork

What You Do:

1. Preheat oven to 300 degrees Fahrenheit.

2. Grease the baking dish with butter.

3. In the saucepan, add milk, half & half, and cornmeal. Stir over medium heat until thickened.

4. In the bowl, whip the eggs with a fork. Add to the hot cornmeal mixture. Stir until well blended.

5. Stir in molasses.

6. Pour into baking dish.

7. Bake uncovered for 45 minutes. Serve warm.

Not every turkey gets roasted
on Thanksgiving.

The president **pardons** at least one lucky turkey each year. It goes to live on a farm.

Many people enjoy the Macy's Thanksgiving Day Parade. Huge balloons march in this New York parade.

Families also watch football games on Thanksgiving. They are thankful to be together!

Glossary

colony—a group of people who have settled in a new place

cornucopia—a horn-shaped basket stuffed with fruits and vegetables; cornucopias are common Thanksgiving decorations.

festival—a celebration

harvest—a time to gather crops

national—related to the entire country

pardons—forgives and sets free

Pilgrims—a group of settlers who came to North America in 1620 on the *Mayflower*

venison—deer meat

Wampanoag—native people from the New England area; *Wampanoag* is pronounced wahm-peh-NO-ahg.

THE MAYFLOWER
1620

To Learn More

AT THE LIBRARY

Bruchac, Joseph. *Squanto's Journey: The Story of the First Thanksgiving*. San Diego, Calif.: Silver Whistle, 2000.

Cunningham, Kevin. *The Wampanoag*. New York, N.Y.: Children's Press, 2011.

Devlin, Wende and Harry. *Cranberry Thanksgiving*. Cynthiana, Ky.: Purplehouse Press, 2012.

ON THE WEB
Learning more about Thanksgiving is as easy as 1, 2, 3.

1. Go to www.factsurfer.com.

2. Enter "Thanksgiving" into the search box.

3. Click the "Surf" button and you will see a list of related web sites.

With factsurfer.com, finding more information is just a click away.

Index